Reader's Digest READING SKILL BUILDER

SILVER EDITION EDITORS

Miriam Weiss Meyer and Peter Travers, Project Editors

Judith Hatch and Victoria Heller, Editors

SILVER EDITION CONSULTANTS

Fred Chavez, Director of Programs
Los Angeles City Reading Support Services Center
Los Angeles, California

Marguerite E. Fuller, Assistant Supervisor of Language Arts
Norwalk Public Schools
Norwalk, Connecticut

Sister Maria Loyola, I.H.M., Chairperson, Reading Curriculum Committee
Archdiocese of Philadelphia
Philadelphia, Pennsylvania

Dr. John. F. Savage, Coordinator, Reading Specialist Program
Boston College, School of Education
Chestnut Hill, Massachusetts

Richard B. Solymos, Reading Resource Teacher
School Board of Broward County
Fort Lauderdale, Florida

READER'S DIGEST EDUCATIONAL DIVISION
© 1977 by Reader's Digest Services, Inc., Pleasantville, N.Y. 10570. All rights reserved, including
the right to reproduce this book or parts thereof in any form.
Printed in the United States of America.
Reader's Digest ® Trademark Reg. U.S. Pat. Off. Marca Registrada ISBN 0-88300-417-8

■■■■ **Part 3**   *Silver Edition*

CONTENTS

Stories for which Audio Lessons are available.
RDX number indicates RDX card for that story.

The Ape that "Talks" with People

by Emily and Ola d'Aulaire

The room looks like the inside of a space-ship. Racks of many-colored push buttons glow softly. The buttons have strange signs on them. Several small screens stretch across the top of the keyboards.

Inside the room is a young chimpanzee named Lana. She punches the push buttons and glances up at the screens. Then she checks the sentence she has written. Then she waits for an answer. Lana is "talking" to the people in the next room.

The next room is divided from the first by a large glass window and sliding glass door. Jammed inside are more keyboards, screens and a computerized language machine. Duane M. Rumbaugh and Timothy V. Gill use them all to study Lana.

The machine has been set up with its own "language" of 255 "words." The words are made up by using nine different signs—a circle, a square, a wavy line, and so forth. Up to four of these signs are joined to make each word. Seven colored backgrounds are used for different kinds of words. Red is for food and drink, violet for people, blue for action. Only words of certain classes can follow others. They must make sense.

When the machine was set up in February 1972, two-year-old Lana was brought into her new home. First Tim showed her the keyboard. She saw how the buttons lit up when pushed. She quickly learned which sign made what happen. Punching "M & M" (her

favorite candy) made one drop into her bowl. "Water" brought her a drink every time.

Then the machine was changed. Lana had to punch "please" before and a dot after each request. "Please" told the machine that Lana was about to ask for something. The dot showed that Lana had finished asking.

One after another, new and different words were added to build sentences. Soon, when Lana wanted candy, she had to punch "Please machine give M&M."

The machine had been set up to show the words, from left to right, on the screens over the keyboard. Would Lana learn to "read" these signs sent her by Tim in the other room? The answer turned out to be yes.

First Rumbaugh and Gill noticed that Lana had begun to glance up at the screens as she pressed each key. Sometimes she would make a mistake punching out her sentence. Lana would catch the mistake on the screens. She would punch the dot button right away. This cleared the screen and keyboard.

Lana began making up new sentences. One day Tim showed Lana a small box filled with candies. "Box" was one of several new

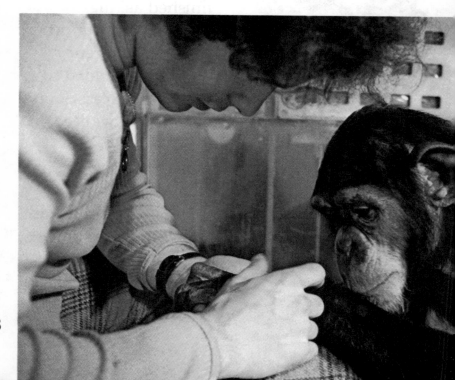

words added to Lana's keyboard that morning. Lana hurried to the keyboard. She asked for the box first as "bowl," then as "can," words she already knew. When these failed, Lana wrote: "Tim give Lana name-of-this."

"Box name-of-this," Tim answered. Lana shot back: "Tim give Lana this box."

No one had ever expected the chimp to ask this kind of question. "There is no question," says Rumbaugh, "that she knows exactly what she is doing."

Indeed. During our visit, Lana asked the machine for milk. Tim used his keyboard to slip incorrect words into the middle of Lana's sentence. Each time Lana would hit the dot button and begin again. Then she decided it was we who were causing the delay. After staring at us in a pointed way, she wrote: "Please move outside of room."

As Tim led us into the hallway, we heard the machine click and hum. Above Tim's empty keyboard, a string of colored screens lit up: "Please machine give milk."

PUNCH IT OUT *signals/antecedents*

Write A before each sentence punctuated correctly according to the article. Write B before each sentence that is not.

___ 1. First Tim showed her the keyboard.

___ 2. Water brought her a drink every time.

___ 3. Lana, had to punch "please" before and a dot after each request.

___ 4. One after another, new and different words were added to build sentences.

___ 5. When these failed, Lana wrote: "Tim give Lana, name-of-this."

☞ 128 • Each correct answer 5 points • My Score ___

TALK TO ME *skimming*

Underline the right sentence ending.

1. The room looks like the inside of a (a. cage, b. kitchen, c. spaceship).
2. The words are made up by using nine different (a. signs, b. sounds, c. songs).
3. Violet is for (a. grapes, b. flowers, c. people).
4. The word showed up on screens above the (a. floor, b. window, c. keyboard).
5. Lana began making up new (a. sentences, b. machines, c. menus).

☞ 135 • Each correct answer 5 points • My Score ___

STUDY THE ANSWERS   *phrase meaning*

Circle the best meaning for the italicized words in each sentence.

1. Racks of many-colored push buttons *glow softly*.
     a. sparkle   b. shine dimly   c. hum

2. They must *make sense*.
     a. be small   b. mean something
     c. ask questions

3. Lana would *catch the mistake* on the screens.
     a. touch the keys   b. find the error
     c. lose the problem

4. She stared at us *in a pointed way*.
     a. blankly   b. sleepily   c. hard

5. Above Tim's keyboard, *a string of* colored screens lit up.
     a. a couple of   b. a series of   c. empty

↜136 · Each correct answer 10 points · My Score _____
Perfect Total Score 100 · My Total Score _____

NAME OF THIS   *vocabulary*

Pretend that you don't know the word "car." Think of other words to replace it in a sentence.

Bamboo: Wood

In the steaming rain forests of Borneo, an island in the Pacific Ocean, Dayak headhunters use it to carry water. In China people cut it up, fry it and eat it. People in Japan and Thailand fashion it into lovely fans and flutes. What is it? Bamboo, the world's most wonderful wood.

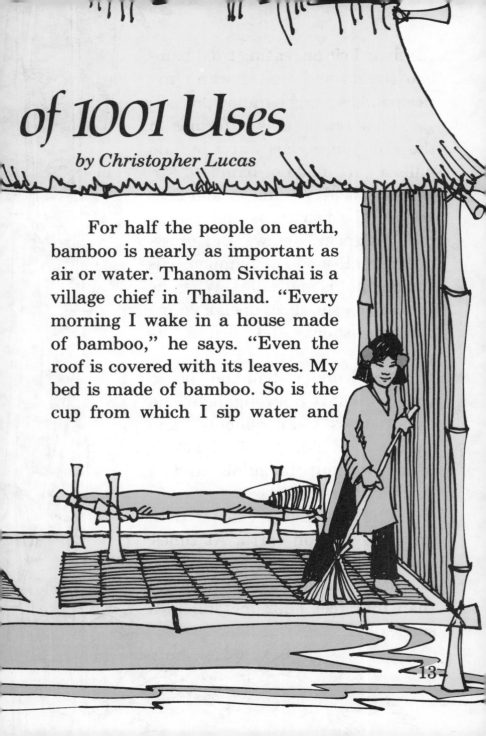

of 1001 Uses

by Christopher Lucas

For half the people on earth, bamboo is nearly as important as air or water. Thanom Sivichai is a village chief in Thailand. "Every morning I wake in a house made of bamboo," he says. "Even the roof is covered with its leaves. My bed is made of bamboo. So is the cup from which I sip water and the floor I sit on, eating fried bamboo shoots and rice. I water my rice paddies using bamboo pipes."

Luis Lualhati is a farmer in the Philippines. His water buffalo pulls a cart made of bamboo. Mr. Lualhati is also a hunter and fisherman. His fish traps and fishing rod, his spear, arrows and crossbow are all made of bamboo. His cooking pot is made of it. When he gets thirsty, he slices open a young bamboo shoot and drinks its water.

No wonder bamboo is so widely used. It is strong, light and cheap. It is clean, smooth, and shiny. It is hollow, it floats, it bends without breaking, and it doesn't wear out.

This wood grows faster than anything else on earth. At times, one can <u>see</u> it grow, for bamboo has been known to push up more than four feet (1.22 meters) in a single day!

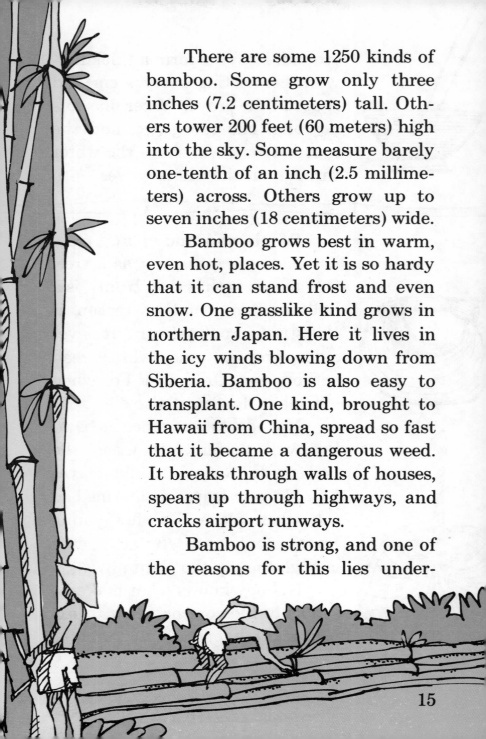

There are some 1250 kinds of bamboo. Some grow only three inches (7.2 centimeters) tall. Others tower 200 feet (60 meters) high into the sky. Some measure barely one-tenth of an inch (2.5 millimeters) across. Others grow up to seven inches (18 centimeters) wide.

Bamboo grows best in warm, even hot, places. Yet it is so hardy that it can stand frost and even snow. One grasslike kind grows in northern Japan. Here it lives in the icy winds blowing down from Siberia. Bamboo is also easy to transplant. One kind, brought to Hawaii from China, spread so fast that it became a dangerous weed. It breaks through walls of houses, spears up through highways, and cracks airport runways.

Bamboo is strong, and one of the reasons for this lies under-

ground. Its roots form a thick network connecting every stem and shoot in the grove. Water one corner of a bamboo grove, and the root network will share the water throughout the whole grove.

People who study plants class bamboo as a grass, not as a tree. One reason is that the "trunk" is a hollow stem. Another reason is this strange root network. It never stops growing and will spread without end. Or almost. For when a bamboo flowers, it also dies.

Nobody knows when a bamboo will flower. Yet when the flowers do come, the old leaves fall. No new leaves are formed to take their place. The few young leaves that are left are never enough to keep the plant alive.

Nobody knows what makes it suddenly blossom or when to expect it. It happens only rarely—

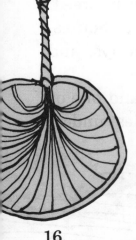

16

sometimes only every 60, or even 120, years. But it is always the same. First one, single plant flowers. Then, over a year or two, the whole grove bursts into small white flowers. Then it dies.

Bamboo grows best in the Orient, where it is most widely used. Its history is closely connected with the histories of the peoples of the Orient. In China the earliest paper was made from bamboo, as were the brushes used for writing and painting. And for over 2000 years, it has been a popular subject of Chinese art.

In China bamboo is called one of the Three Friends. It stands for one of the three great wise men of China's history, Buddha. Here, as in all of Asia, bamboo—the wood with 1001 uses—stands for happiness and good fortune.

CUT OUT THE ANSWER *supporting details*

Underline the words that best complete each sentence.

1. Bamboo is widely used because it is (a. hard and thick, b. hollow and bends, c. expensive and rare).

2. There are some (a. 50, b. 1250, c. 2500) kinds of bamboo.

3. Bamboo grows best in (a. frozen, b. warm, c. faraway) places.

4. People who study plants class bamboo as a (a. tree, b. vine, c. grass).

5. When a bamboo flowers, it also (a. grows, b. dies, c. multiplies).

☞136 • *Each correct answer 10 points* • *My Score* _____

CHECK THIS *classification/outline*

In the story, the author calls bamboo "the wood with 1001 uses." What do you remember about bamboo? Check ✓ five uses for bamboo.

_____1. tires   _____5. pipes
_____2. food   _____6. houses
_____3. radios   _____7. glass
_____4. flutes   _____8. fishing rods

☞170 • *Each correct answer 5 points* • *My Score* _____

LET'S SEE IT   *story elements*

Underline the word or words used by the author to paint the more exact picture.

1. In the (a. hot, b. steaming) rain forests of Borneo, an island in the Pacific Ocean, Dayak headhunters use it to carry water.

2. When he gets thirsty, he (a. slices, b. cuts) open a young bamboo shoot and drinks its water.

3. Bamboo has been known to (a. grow, b. push up) more than four feet in a single day.

4. Others (a. tower, b. stand) 200 feet high into the sky.

5. Some (a. measure, b. are) barely one-tenth of an inch across.

☞ 130 • Each correct answer 5 points • My Score ____
Perfect Total Score 100 • My Total Score ____

YOUR TURN   *comparison/contrast*

Have you ever had anything made of bamboo? Can you think of bamboo objects not mentioned in the story? Give examples.

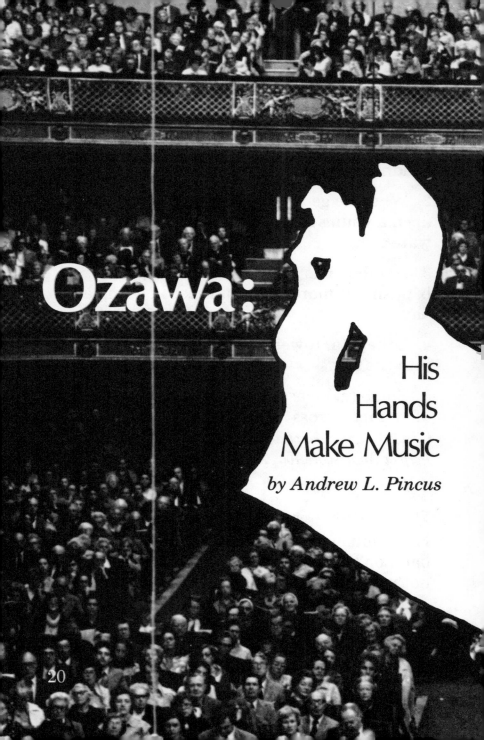

Ozawa:

His Hands Make Music

by Andrew L. Pincus

Seiju Ozawa (SAY-gee o-ZAH-wah) had his 40th birthday not long ago. There are streaks of gray in his flowing black hair. He no longer bursts onto the stage like a child bounding out of school. But age has increased his musical powers. He is one of the best orchestra conductors in the world.

"When I turned 20, that was a shock," says Mr. Ozawa. "I was living in Japan and

21

had no money. At that time, people thought it was impossible for a Japanese to lead a big orchestra. So 40, that's no shock." Now, neither is his leading the Boston Symphony Orchestra a shock.

Ozawa's life in Japan helped make him a serious conductor. He was born in China. His father was a dentist. The family moved to Japan, and Ozawa attended the Toho School of Music in Tokyo. He had been studying piano since he was seven. But in Tokyo he broke two fingers playing rugby. That ended his career as a pianist.

Ozawa decided to become a conductor. So he began serious training with orchestras in Japan. That training taught him great control and helped him learn how to reach the heart of a piece of music. However, when he came to the United States in 1960, he could barely speak English. Musicians who played under him remember how he used his body instead of words to get his ideas across. Many people, watching him conduct the orchestra, say he moves like a dancer.

To audiences, Ozawa shows growth in how he behaves at the podium. In the begin-

ning, he was painfully shy. When the audience applauded, he thought he didn't deserve it. Now he bows gracefully to his cheering public. There is a sense of knowing his own worth. He is like the captain of a winning team.

Even though he is a music superstar, Ozawa doesn't like to talk much about music. His friends know he is charming and warm. But he doesn't like to speak before an au-

dience. Instead he gives out autographs so freely that friends have to tell him when to stop.

Ozawa's English has gotten much better. Still he prefers to let his conducting speak for him. He says that music with words—choral music—is his biggest problem. But he can easily handle a group of 300 singers. He weaves their voices with those of the instruments. It becomes a beautiful cloth of sound. Each vocal and instrumental line is clear.

Ozawa sees a piece of music as a whole. Other conductors spend a lot of time worrying about small things. The leader of one section of the orchestra says he has to do a lot of work with his players between rehearsals.

The section leader calls it "sweeping up the crumbs."

Off the podium, Ozawa has always loved sports. He plays them with the same care that he brings to his work. His favorite sports are snow skiing and water skiing. And he is taking tennis lessons. "I love lessons," he says. "I think it has something to do with being a musician. You always want to be taking lessons."

So life is good for Ozawa. He is doing exactly what he always wanted to do. And he is doing it better than almost anyone. Of his broken fingers, he once said, "I wanted to be a really good rugby player, at the highest level." That's how he does everything. At the highest level.

KEEP THE TIME *sequence*

Number four steps in Ozawa's life from 1 to 4.

_____ He came to the United States in 1960.

_____ Ozawa went to school in Tokyo.

_____ He was born in China.

_____ He began studying piano at seven.

☞ *105 • Each correct answer 5 points • My Score* _____

PLAY IT AGAIN *vocabulary*

From the list of words, choose one word to match each clue below. Write the letter of the word in the blank before the clue.

Words

a. conductor   c. violin

b. symphony   d. podium

Clues

_____ 1. piece of music for an orchestra

_____ 2. musical instrument with four strings

_____ 3. a raised platform

_____ 4. leader of an orchestra

☞ *103 • Each correct answer 5 points • My Score* _____

PICTURE THIS *author's purpose*

To send you a good word-picture of Ozawa, which six of the following phrases did the author use? Check ✔ each.

_____ 1. flowing black hair

26

_____ 2. music superstar
_____ 3. a dentist
_____ 4. captain of winning team
_____ 5. moves like a dancer
_____ 6. charming and warm
_____ 7. sweeping up the crumbs
_____ 8. great control

☞ *215 • Each correct answer 5 points • My Score* _____

ZERO IN *sentence meaning*

Ozawa said the following words. What do they show about how he felt or acted? Circle a, b, or c.

1. "When I turned 20, that was a shock."
   a. happy   b. surprised   c. tired

2. "You always want to be taking lessons."
   a. angry   b. funny   c. ambitious

3. "I wanted to be a really good rugby player."
   a. disappointed   b. lazy   c. scared

☞ *52 • Each correct answer 10 points • My Score* _____
Perfect Total Score 100 • My Total Score _____

VARIATION ON A THEME *main idea*

Reread this story. Which paragraph best explains what the main idea of the story is? Be sure to give reasons for your answer.

Count Dracula

The Fiend You Love to Hate

by James Stewart-Gordon

It was a stormy night with the moon low in the sky. A tall, thin man appeared. He looked like a giant bat. His black cape floated from his shoulders. He leaned closer to the lovely dark-haired woman. Then he drew back his lips from his shiny white teeth. Eyes wide, the woman waited. "My dear," he whispered, "I'd love to give you my autograph." He took a slip of paper from her fingers. He wrote "Count Dracula" across it and handed it back. Then the woman fainted.

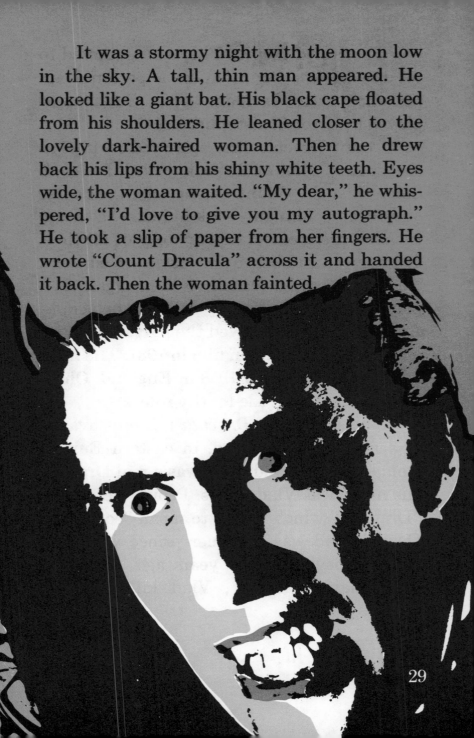

The crowd gasped. They had gathered to see the ageless Count make a personal appearance near London. This Count was played by actor Christopher Lee.

Count Dracula first appeared in 1897 as the spooky star of a book called *Dracula*. Since then the Count has become the center of a theater, film and book industry. *Dracula* is called the greatest horror story of all time. It has been published in dozens of editions. The story can be read in 44 languages. As a play, it has been seen by millions of people. Actor Bela Lugosi played the part in America on stage in 1927 and on film in 1931. The movie was made again in 1958 in England. Christopher Lee played the toothy role.

The setting for *Dracula* is Transylvania, now a part of Romania, in eastern Europe. Romanians believed there was a real Dracula. His name was Vlad Tepes. People called him "Dracula," which is said to mean "son of the Devil." Vlad was a former prince who lived near Transylvania 500 years ago. According to Romanian history, Vlad killed 100,000 people.

Vlad Tepes ▶

The fictional Dracula was created by Bram (short for Abraham) Stoker. Stoker was a flame-bearded Irishman, born in Dublin in 1847. He had served in the Irish Civil Service as a court clerk. Later he became general manager of a London theatrical company. He also found time to become a lawyer. As a writer, he turned out five books and several stories. His most famous book was the tale of the Count, based on folklore he had heard.

Transylvania was chosen as the setting because it sounded mysterious. Stoker made Borgo Pass, another real place, the spot from which the hero, Jonathan Harker, sets out to

Bela Lugosi strikes terror as Count Dracula

meet the Count. That's how the great story begins. It follows the Count's bloody trail to Carfax, a run-down estate near London.

Someone asked Stoker how he thought of the idea. "Well," he replied, "I had a dish of crab one night. Then I had a nightmare. Then I wrote the book." In reality he worked at it during summer vacations in Scotland.

Hamilton Deane, a friend of Stoker's, wrote the play that became a hit in 1927 in London. He had an idea that helped its success. Deane hired a nurse to walk up and down the theater aisles during the performance. That way, if someone fainted, he or she would have medical help. One evening 29 people in the theater fainted. After that, to see the play was a test of nerves.

Not long ago I drove from London to Essex. In the book, that's where Carfax is. It was there that the Count lived and scared England. After dinner I walked out to the edge of town. I knew that make-believe Carfax should be on my left.

Mist covered the road. Then the fog thinned. A single fluttering object swooped through the pale moonlight. A bat! I turned and ran back to town. I fled to my hotel room and locked the door. My heart was pounding, and I thought of a line from the Dracula play, "Sleep well."

Seeing Dracula on stage, screen or television will go on making that impossible for generations of readers. But what horror movie fan would have it any other way?

WHAT COUNTS? *supporting details*

Circle the letter of the ending that would help you recall a fact.

1. Count Dracula first appeared in a book in (a. 1640, b. 1700, c. 1897).

2. The book was written by (a. Bram Stoker, b. Bela Lugosi, c. Christopher Lee).

3. The main setting for Dracula is (a. China, b. Italy, c. Romania).

4. Vlad Tepes was a (a. writer, b. movie star, c. former prince).

5. Hamilton Deane (a. wrote the play, b. starred in the film, c. produced the film).

☞135 • *Each correct answer 5 points* • *My Score* _____

SCARED YET? *characterization*

Five of the words below describe Count Dracula. Circle each of the words.

1. thin   5. ageless
2. blond   6. funny
3. tall   7. spooky
4. toothy   8. cheerful

☞171 • *Each correct answer 10 points* • *My Score* _____

WHAT DOES IT MEAN? *story elements*

The author wrote each group of italicized

words to create a mood. Underline the sentence that means nearly the same thing.

1. *Then he drew back his lips from his shiny white teeth.*
   a. He started biting.
   b. He smiled.

2. *He turned out five books.*
   a. He wrote five books.
   b. He threw away five books.

3. *To see the play was a test of nerves.*
   a. The play was boring.
   b. If you didn't faint, you were brave.

4. *A single fluttering object swooped through the pale moonlight.*
   a. Something flew by at night.
   b. Nothing moved in the darkness.

5. *My heart was pounding.*
   a. I was scared stiff.
   b. I was sick.

⟜130 • Each correct answer 5 points • My Score ____
Perfect Total Score 100 • My Total Score ____

SWEET DREAMS *summary*

Do you think the title of the story is a good one? Think of another title that would summarize the story.

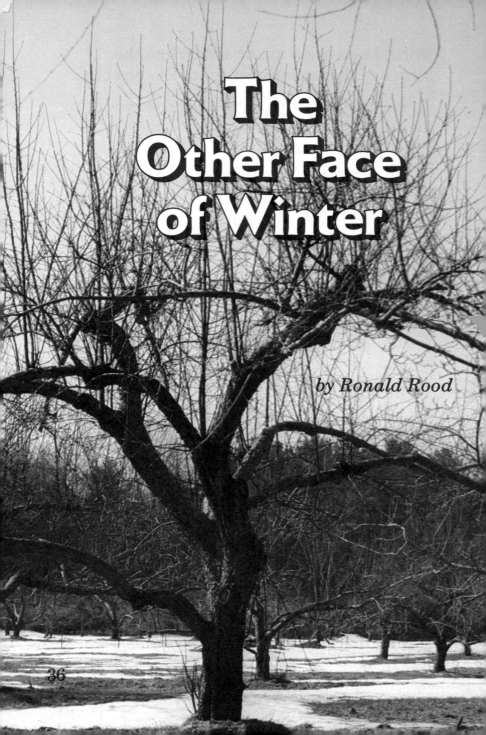

The Other Face of Winter

by Ronald Rood

A friend from Florida praised an apple orchard near our Vermont home so much that I sent him a couple of little McIntosh trees. That was 13 years ago. Last summer I asked how they were doing.

"Oh, fine," he told me. "They're 20 feet (6.1 meters) tall. But when do I get any apples?"

I hated to tell him. Those trees are not likely to bear fruit. Apple trees cannot make fruit unless they have between 900 and 1000 hours of cold weather, below 45°F (7°C).

What my friend's trees have needed is what our Vermont trees get every year: a good, cold sleep. In warm Florida, his trees have been growing themselves to death.

My friend's story isn't surprising. There is something good about winter, no matter what some people say. The lives of many plants and animals depend upon the freezing cold as much as upon warmth. Vermont's well-known sugar maple will grow as far south as the Carolinas. But it will produce very little sap. It takes wild leaps in temperature—from 0° to 40°F (−18°C to 4°C) in a few hours—to make the sap flow. Without such jumps, it often doesn't even color its leaves in the fall. The leaves drop still green.

Many plants could not live in the north if it weren't for winter. A number of seeds, such as ash, wild plum and black oak, won't begin to grow until they've had a cold period. Pine

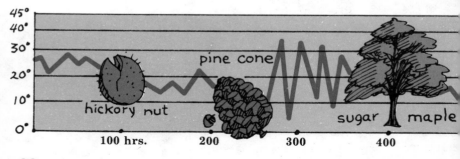

38

cones open and close a tiny bit as it gets warmer and colder. This is what allows the seeds to drop. The shells of hickory nuts swell and break open as the winter frost works at their seams. By spring the once-hard shell is weakened. Then the growing plant inside can break out.

Winter's time clock controls buds, too. If you pick some maple or cherry branches in winter hoping to force them to early bloom indoors, you'll have little luck. But if you wait until late March or April, they'll blossom beautifully. By then their winter sleep is nearly done.

Thousands of northern birds, fish, mammals, insects and worms stay alive in winter. They find it more friend than enemy. In creeks and along pond edges, geese and ducks have little trouble with winter's cold. The key is their double suit of feathers. The outside

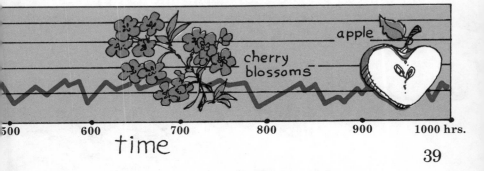

cherry
blossoms

apple

500   600   700   800   900   1000 hrs.

time

feathers overlap like slate on a roof. These feathers cut wind and water. The soft, thick feathers underneath serve as snug insulation.

Snow is a big help, too. The ground below the surface of a snow drift is much warmer than the air above. Deer and moose often bed down for a night in the snow in a sheltered spot. Some game birds dive full-speed into a snowdrift. They remain there while the storm whistles above.

Field mice tunnel through this quiet world. They are hidden by the warming cover, safe from a host of enemies. The same snow covers the low-growing berries and bushes. It serves to fresh-freeze small fruit and leaves until spring. They are eaten when animals that have slept all winter awaken and need such food.

Insects and spiders in the soil lie in the cold as stiff as plastic toys. Dig out a spider from beneath a piece of bark, and it appears

dead. But warm it in your hands for a moment, and it springs to life. Break a rotten log, and hundreds of carpenter ants tumble out like black seeds.

Why don't these tiny things freeze when it's well below zero? These ants make glycerol in their bodies. It is something like what is used in automobile radiators to keep them from freezing in winter. The ant's body stops making glycerol when summer comes.

Many animals sleep through the season, though some sleep more deeply than others. A woodchuck in winter can be dug out of his den and rolled across the floor without waking up. But don't try that with a black bear!

People may go south if they want to. But for many things of the north, the blasts of winter really are friendly breezes. These wild things are often brought to their best through struggle and hard times.

NAME IT *vocabulary*

From the list below, choose the word that fits each definition. Write the letter in the space provided.

a. sap
b. depend
c. weakened
d. insulation
e. glycerol

____ antifreeze for bugs
____ tree liquid from which maple sugar is made
____ rely
____ protection against loss of body heat
____ made less strong

155 • Each correct answer 5 points • My Score ____

THE COLD FACTS *paragraph meaning*

Write A before each of the sentences below that would make a paragraph about how plants and animals react to winter. Write B before each sentence that would not.

____ 1. Apple trees cannot make fruit unless they have between 900 and 1000 hours of cold weather below 45°F.

____ 2. I sent an apple tree to Florida 13 years ago.

____ 3. My friend's story isn't surprising.

____ 4. Many plants depend upon cold.

____ 5. The leaves drop still green.

128 • Each correct answer 5 points • My Score ____

COLD ENOUGH FOR YOU? *cause/effect*

Put the letter of the plant or animal beside the description of what winter does to it.

a. hickory nut   ____ 1. makes it sleepy
b. maple tree   ____ 2. cracks its shell
c. berry   ____ 3. helps produce sap
d. insects   ____ 4. become stiff
e. woodchuck   ____ 5. fresh-freezes it

☞155 • *Each correct answer 5 points* • *My Score* ____

SMALL TALK *author's purpose*

Write A if the author wanted to tell *how,* B if he wanted to tell *when,* and C if he wanted to tell *where.*

____ 1. beautifully   ____ 4. along pond
____ 2. last summer   edges
____ 3. in warm Florida   ____ 5. friendly

☞ 133 • *Each correct answer 5 points* • *My Score* ____
Perfect Total Score 100 • *My Total Score* ____

THE OTHER SIDE *summary*

Read the last paragraph on page 38, which begins, "Many plants could not live in the north . . . ." Which sentence in the paragraph best sums up the meaning of the article?

44

Manuel Orantes

Gentleman of the Court

by Raul Vázques de Parga

It was the quarter finals of the U.S. Open at Forest Hills in 1975. This was one of the biggest matches in tennis. Romania's Ilie Nastase (EE-lee na-STAH-zee) had just served to Spain's Manuel Orantes (man-WELL o-RAN-tays). The umpire and linesman couldn't agree whether the ball went in the court or out. But Orantes knew the shot was good. The point was played over. Orantes walked away from the ball, which cost him the set. Later he said, "I don't like to win because the linesman made a mistake." Being a good sport has made Orantes one of the best-liked tennis players.

Orantes is one of the best tennis players alive. In 1975 he won eight major titles in tennis matches all over the world. He earned over a quarter of a million dollars in winnings. Becoming a champion wasn't easy.

Orantes was born in 1949 in Spain. His mother died when he was six months old. Orantes lived with his father and two brothers in a hut in Barcelona, one of Spain's largest cities. Their home had no running water or electricity. But it was near the La Salud Tennis Club. There Orantes became a ballboy at age ten.

Within a year, Orantes was beating members of the Pee Wee team in pickup games. The kid with the borrowed tennis racquet could really play. Soon the coach asked him to join the team. Orantes was given tennis lessons. He got free meals from the club's kitchen and an education at a local school.

In 1964 Orantes was coached by Juan Ventura. Ventura would shout, "This is not play! This is your work! Tennis could be your future!" Orantes didn't believe it, not until another former ballboy from Spain became a tennis star. Manuel Santana won the world's biggest tennis matches.

If it could happen to Santana, it could happen to Orantes. So Orantes dug in. He began piling up trophies. And in 1968, he beat Santana himself.

Being a professional tennis player can be a lonely business. It means going around the world meeting new people. But Orantes was shy. He had only been to high school. So he

learned how to speak English, French and Italian. He started to read up on world news. Slowly he gained confidence.

One thing Orantes couldn't shrug off was a back problem. In 1972 he couldn't bend over to tie his shoes. His doctors ordered him off the courts for six months. When he returned to tennis, he could no longer whip his body into the ball. He was forced to develop a wooden-soldier serve, putting all his power into his arm. He had a good season in 1974, but his back suddenly weakened.

Orantes decided to see another doctor. The doctor said that Orantes' right side was weaker than his left. So Orantes was given a set of exercises to do every day for 90 minutes. The back trouble cleared up.

When he got to the 1975 Forest Hills match, Orantes felt he had as good a chance as anyone to win. Everyone was making a fuss over the tennis superstars. Favorites were Arthur Ashe, Guillermo Vilas and

Jimmy Connors. Orantes neatly defeated all comers. The last match was against champion Connors. When Orantes walked onto the court, he was cool against the fiery Connors. He won every game. Even Connors said, "He played unbelievably."

People said that Orantes was like Santana. "I don't compare myself to anyone," Orantes says. "I'm just me."

For fans who like great tennis from a good sport, that's good enough.

LINE IT UP *sequence*

Number in order the events in Manuel Orantes' life. One numeral is put in to help you. You may refer back to the article.

__2__ Orantes lived with his father and two brothers in a hut in Barcelona.

____ Orantes was born in 1949 in Spain.

____ In 1964 Orantes was coached by Juan Ventura.

____ Orantes was given tennis lessons.

____ Orantes became a ballboy at the club at age ten.

____ Within a year, Orantes was beating members of the Pee Wee team.

☞ *210 · Each correct answer 5 points · My Score* ____

THINK ABOUT IT *characterization*

Which five words or phrases help you see Orantes in your mind? Check ✔ each.

____ 1. umpire

____ 2. good sport

____ 3. coach

____ 4. good manners

____ 5. shy

____ 6. back trouble

____ 7. nervous

____ 8. cool

☞ *170 · Each correct answer 5 points · My Score* ____

ACE IT   *fact/opinion*

Read each sentence below. Put A before each sentence that is fact. Put B before each sentence that says what the author believes but may not be fact.

_____ Being a professional tennis player can be a lonely business.

_____ It was the quarter finals of the U.S. Open at Forest Hills in 1975.

_____ Slowly he gained confidence.

_____ In 1972 he couldn't bend over to tie his shoes.

_____ Orantes was given a set of exercises to do every day for 90 minutes.

☞ *130 · Each correct answer 10 points · My Score* _____

Perfect Total Score 100 · My Total Score _____

YOUR SERVE   *generalizations*

Do you think the title "Manuel Orantes: Gentleman of the Court" is a good one?

What is a gentleman? What is a lady? Give examples from the story and from your life.

PIED PIPER OF

It is rush hour in a New York City subway station as a train covered with writing jerks to a stop. Its doors open with a hiss, and I push on board. Forty fellow robots hide their faces behind newspapers. They seem to say, "Please don't bother us."

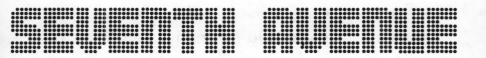

SEVENTH AVENUE

by James Comer

There's an empty seat—a miracle. As I sit down, my eye strays to the man on my right. Now I know why this seat was empty.

He looks all right, but his shirt and pants need cleaning. It's not his clothes that make me nervous; it's what he's doing. He's holding

a gray typewriter case between his knees. He pulls out a pair of old drumsticks and gets to work. His eyes look at an invisible conductor as he begins to play the case as though it were a drum. At first I want to move away, but he wins me over by his style.

I've always been a pencil-thumper, so I know what a good beat is. The man is not just interesting, he's a good musician. Sounds fly and the beat changes quickly—fast, then

slow, then fast again. He drops a stick, picks it up and looks at it closely to see if it is broken. It isn't.

Tap! Tap! Tap! He begins again.

What a show! He pounds away, flipping one stick, then the other, high over his head. Surely he will miss—no, he catches them both easily.

He is an artist and knows he's good. He doesn't seem to notice people around him. No

one offers him money, and he doesn't ask for any.

Finally I notice the other people on the train. Sourpusses no more! I see about me a group of happy, laughing faces—smiles for miles, feet tapping, heads keeping time. The people in the subway car have become friends, if only for a few station stops.

Our nameless drummer has done all this, and it took fewer than five minutes. At the

next stop, he quietly gathers his things and gets off the train. Is he a musician or is he just odd? Is he an out-of-work genius, too poor to buy a drum? I don't know. I like to remember him as the Pied Piper of Seventh Avenue.

And my smile lasts all the way home.

DRUM UP THE ANSWER *supporting details*

Underline the right ending for each sentence.

1. The "Pied Piper" in the article is a
   a. conductor.   b. drummer.   c. writer.

2. The "Pied Piper" looks
   a. neat.   b. well dressed.   c. messy.

3. Most of the article takes place on a
   a. subway train.   b. street.   c. trolley.

4. When the writer first saw the "Pied Piper,"
the writer became
   a. very angry.   b. kind of nervous.
   c. cheerful and happy.

☞ *90 • Each correct answer 5 points • My Score* ____

EDUCATED GUESS *phrase meaning*

The author gives clues to the meaning of each
italicized phrase below. Circle the letter of the
meaning.

1. A train covered with writing *jerks to a
stop*.
   a. halts suddenly   b. stops slowly
   c. gets stuck

2. Forty *fellow robots* hide their faces behind
newspapers.
   a. club members   b. noisy children
   c. machinelike people

58

3. His eyes look at an *imaginary conductor.*
   a. hidden fare collector
   b. tracks under the train
   c. make-believe orchestra leader

4. I've always been a *pencil-thumper.*
   a. story-teller   b. untrained drummer
   c. artist's assistant

☞89 · *Each correct answer 10 points* · *My Score* _____

TRACK THE FACTS   *characterization*

Which four facts help you picture the Pied
Piper in your mind? Underline each.

1. His clothes are dirty.
2. He's holding a gray typewriter case.
3. There's an empty seat next to him.
4. He pulls out a pair of old drumsticks
   and gets to work.
5. At first I want to move away.
6. He pounds away, flipping one stick,
   then the other, high over his head.

☞ 123 · *Each correct answer 10 points* · *My Score* _____
Perfect Total Score 100 · *My Total Score* _____

STREET SAVVY   *story elements*

What words did the author use to describe
the sound of the Pied Piper's "drum"? What
other words can you make up to describe it?

The Fairest Cape

by W. A. de Klerk
photographs by Terence McNally

Table Mountain. *This mountain forms a huge background for the city of Cape Town. A mass of blue-gray sandstone, it rises 3609 feet (1100 meters).* Botanists *(people who study plants) have found more kinds of plants here than on all the British Isles.*

Cape Point. Below Vasco da Gama Peak are sandstone cliffs. The building here is Cape Point lighthouse.

61

Orange River Cataract. Nature remains untouched at Aughrabies Falls. It is one of South Africa's most beautiful sights.

I have climbed South Africa's Cape Point to Vasco da Gama Peak. That windy height is some 886 feet (270 meters) above the ocean. Here the waters of the icy Atlantic meet the warm Indian Ocean.

Every time I climb the peak, I remember the words Sir Francis Drake wrote during a trip round the world in the 1500s. "This Cape is the most stately thing," he said, "and the fairest Cape we saw . . ." Drake was talking about the whole peninsula. It is a small corner of the greater Province of the Cape of Good Hope. South Africans call it the Cape.

The first European set foot on the Cape in 1488. His name was Bartholomew Dias, and he was a Portuguese sailor. Early sailors thought they had found the sea route to India. That's why it was named the Cape of Good Hope. It was Vasco da Gama who finally made the passage to India. The Cape became a natural *staging post* (stopping place) between West and East.

When I stand on Da Gama Peak, I have a vision of this whole vast land. Here are six pictures of the Cape I especially cherish.

The Great Karoo. The Great Karoo is the biggest plateau outside of Asia and forms half of the Cape Province. "Karoo" comes from an African word meaning dry and sparsely covered. South Africa produces its finest wools from sheep that graze here. Sometimes there are great droughts, when rain stays away for months or even years. Then the Karoo seems to die. But when the rains return, the desert springs to life.

The Garden Route.
This charming route
crosses one of the most
beautiful landscapes in
Africa. It is filled with
lakes, mountains and
valleys. In the evergreen
Tsitsikamma Forest
are bright streams that
rush to the sea. But
industry may destroy
the Garden Route, so
conservationists are
fighting to protect it. ▶

Cape Dutch Houses. *These houses were designed by the Dutch many years ago. They are seen at their best surrounded by great oaks, lush vineyards and orchards. They blend with the mountains behind that look like castles.*

Berge van die Boland. *This is a view of Du Toit's Kloof. In South Africa,* kloof *means ravine or steep-sided valley. This area is typical of the mountains in the southwestern Cape. There are many peaks, valleys, evergreen forests and streams. The peaks, dressed with snow, attract many mountain climbers. The summer air is as clear as the waters that tumble down a thousand kloofs.*

CHOOSE YOUR WORDS *vocabulary*

Circle the best meaning for each italicized word.

1. In South Africa, *kloof* means (a. steep-sided valley, b. plant life, c. sheep).

2. *Botanists* are people who study (a. geography, b. plants, c. languages).

3. A *landscape* is a (a. map, b. gardening tool, c. view of scenery on land).

4. A *conservationist* is a (a. news reporter, b. businessman, c. protector of nature).

5. *Karoo* comes from an African word meaning (a. dry and sparsely covered, b. large animal, c. rainy season).

☞*133 • Each correct answer 5 points • My Score* ____

MAP OUT THE ANSWER *supporting details*

Underline the word or words that best complete each sentence.

1. Vasco da Gama Peak is some (a. 886, b. 1200, c. 2000) feet above the ocean.

2. Here the waters of the icy Atlantic meet the warm (a. Red Sea, b. Indian Ocean, c. Nile River).

3. The Cape is part of the Province of the Cape of Good (a. Will, b. Hope, c. Luck).

4. Early sailors thought they had found the
(a. sea, b. air, c. land) route to India.

5. It was (a. Columbus, b. Vasco da Gama,
c. the Vikings) who finally made the passage
to India.

☞ *128 • Each correct answer 10 points • My Score* ____

WHICH IS WHICH?   *fact/opinion*

Put A before each sentence that is fact and B
before each that is the author's opinion.

____ 1. The houses seem to grow out of the
very soil of the Cape.

____ 2. The first European set foot on the
Cape in 1488.

____ 3. The Great Karoo forms more than
half of the Cape Province.

____ 4. They blend with the mountains
behind that look like castles.

____ 5. The land once more becomes a delight.

☞ *129 • Each correct answer 5 points • My Score* ____
Perfect Total Score 100 • My Total Score ____

EXPLORE YOUR MIND   *graphics*

Which of the six places pictured would you
like to see most? Give reasons for your
answer.

Out-of-Sight Sounds

by N. R. Kleinfield

"MMMMMMMM ... BZZZZZZ ... MMMMMMM ... BZZZ ... BAP ... POW ... THUD ... UGHHH ... WHAM ... POW ... CRASHHH ... THUD ... "

Here's what you're supposed to have just heard: A quiet restaurant suddenly breaks into a full-scale fight. Punches fly as people chatter away. One fellow is thrown across the room. He slams into a table. Plates and glasses crash. As the man tumbles to the floor, a bomb lands on the roof.

Here's what is really happening: Frank and Tom Valentino are batting a couple of empty mail sacks around with wood clubs in their small studio. Then Frank tosses one of the sacks onto a pile of empty boxes. Meanwhile Chris Carrino fiddles with a tape machine, recording the noise. He then makes it twice as loud. He mixes it with a record of crowd murmurs taken from a movie soundtrack. Finally he adds a recording of a bomb blast.

The Valentino brothers and Chris Carrino are sound-effects experts. They work for a company called Thomas J. Valentino, Inc. It's the oldest (founded in 1932) and largest company of its kind. When you hear non-human sounds on TV, radio, in movies or the-

ater, there's a good chance that they were made at Valentino's in New York City.

The Valentinos will try to reproduce any known sound. Right now they have some 5000 noises in stock. There are rock slides and ape screams. There are people swimming and autos racing. You name it, the Valentinos have it on record.

Thomas Valentino founded the company back when noises were faked by rattling metal sheets, firing popguns and beating tin pans. At first Mr. Valentino owned a small shop where he sold printed music and records. He also ran a booth where people could make their own records to mail to friends.

One day Mr. Valentino thought of a good gift for a friend leaving the country. He would make a record of New York street sounds. Valentino was taping noises on a Manhattan street corner. A stage manager from a Broadway play spotted him. Could he produce an offstage noise of a passing milk wagon? Valentino did, and soon entered the noise business full time. Mr. Valentino's three sons, Bob, Frank and Tom, now run the company. Chris Carrino is the sound engineer.

Many real sounds don't sound real on records. So the Valentinos and Chris Carrino have to create noises for about half the sounds they are asked to make. Frank says, "You have to let your mind run wild. Maybe you'll take a paper bag and turn it into World War II."

The experts failed, for example, to reproduce the sound of a baby crying. Nothing sounded right. Finally they hired a middle-aged woman who made the finest baby cry the Valentinos had ever heard. It was the same with the gorilla noises made by an actor who walked in off the street one afternoon. Chris says, "I swear, I've never heard a better ape in my life."

For one movie, the Valentinos were asked to make the sound of a salad being tossed. Tom went home and tossed lettuce long into the night. No good. The lettuce wasn't fresh enough. So Chris crumpled up a newspaper, watered it and shuffled it around in a cardboard box. It worked, and the movie people used it.

Enough is enough, however. Sometimes customers ask for sounds of clouds and snow. Neither of them has a sound, so the Valentinos politely tell them to forget it. There is no argument. If a sound exists, the Valentinos have it on record.

GOT IT? *skimming*

Underline the sentence ending that will help you recall a fact.

1. The Valentino brothers and Chris Carrino are (a. movie stars, b. radio reporters, c. sound-effects experts).

2. Thomas J. Valentino, Inc., has (a. 5000, b. 6000, c. 7000) noises on record.

3. The company was founded in (a. 1925, b. 1932, c. 1945).

4. Frank Valentino suggested he could take a paper bag and turn it into (a. a box, b. World War II, c. confetti).

5. The company is located in (a. New York City, b. Chicago, c. Los Angeles).

6. Sometimes customers ask for soundless sounds such as (a. flies, b. wind, c. snow).

↩180 • Each correct answer 5 points • My Score _____

LET'S HEAR IT *sentence meaning*

Put 1 before each sentence that describes a feeling. Put 2 before each sentence that describes an action.

_____ 1. Punches fly as people chatter away.
_____ 2. One fellow is thrown across the room.
_____ 3. Chris Carrino, recording the noise, fiddles with a tape machine.

_____ 4. Chris crumpled up a newspaper.

_____ 5. "You have to let your mind run wild."

☞132 • *Each correct answer 10 points* • *My Score* _____

SPEAK UP   *cause/effect*

Write the numeral of the method used by the Valentinos to reproduce the sounds below.

Method
1. crumpling a wet newspaper
2. taping an unknown actor
3. recording a middle-aged woman
4. beating empty mail sacks

Sound
_____ restaurant fight
_____ baby's cry
_____ tossed salad
_____ gorilla noises

☞105 • *Each correct answer 5 points* • *My Score* _____
Perfect Total Score 100 • *My Total Score* _____

SOUND IT OUT   *story elements*

What were soundless sounds described in the article? Can you think of other things that don't make sounds? Give examples.

The Cat That Could

by Era Zistel

He was my cat, but I didn't know him very well. As a kitten, he loved to explore the house and go outside. He was named after Marco Polo, a famous 14th-century traveler. We called him Marco for short.

Marco spent most of his days in the woods in back of our house, but he always came home to eat and sleep. So at least to that extent, he was my cat.

One day I heard the screech of car brakes. I ran out to find him lying in a ditch, his head thrown back, eyes open, unseeing. I put him a cardboard box, thinking he was dead. Then I heard a soft moan.

As best I could, I nursed him until he was on his feet again. I thought he had regained his health, but I was wrong. One afternoon when we were both outside together, I noticed his strange walk—a stiff, careful trot. Marco raised each paw high, then put it forward slowly. I made a sudden noise, and Marco jumped and ran, crashing into a basket that was lying in the path.

Marco was blind.

How long had he been using his paw the way a blind person uses a cane? How often had he gone hungry, unable to see his food? I knew cats had a keen sense of smell, but when given food, Marco didn't know about it until he walked into it. Then I thought of tapping on the floor, a signal he quickly learned meant that food had been put exactly there.

Marco was still an explorer. The first time I saw him on the roof, my heart skipped a beat. He got up, yawned, and walked to the edge of the roof. He waved a paw to find a tree branch, tapped to make certain, then leaped onto it. He walked along the tree branch to the trunk, slid down and calmly strolled over to me.

As his confidence grew, so did his exploring. Soon he was visiting the woods out back again. I'd watch with wonder as he made his way through the trees without ever bumping into anything. Or he'd chase windblown leaves in jerky gallops that made me laugh and almost cry.

He not only knew my voice, he also knew my moods. When I was out of sorts, he knew it and sulked. When I was in a good mood, Marco would be as playful as a kitten.

Years passed, and when he was 12, there were signs of age. He no longer sunned himself on the roof. Instead he would lie in a patch of sunlight near the house. Then when he was 13, something went wrong with his brain. The doctor said it was a stroke, but Marco wasn't about to give up.

Day after day, he worked on his unmoving legs and finally got them to twitch. He tried to stand and fell, tried again and fell. He kept trying until at last he was on his feet, swaying. When he walked, his legs dragged. Every so often he'd flop over—but he was determined. Asking to be let outside, he'd fall down the steps, pick himself up and go where he had made up his mind to go.

In his 15th year, he changed even more. Now, instead of lying in the sun, he looked toward the woods and howled. He couldn't get there by himself, so I had to help him.

Crossing the brook was a problem. I tried carrying him, but he wanted to be independent, even though he couldn't find the stepping stones. I tried the tapping trick again, as I had with the food. I slapped a foot down on each stone so he could follow the sound.

My wish was that the end would come for him there, in the woods, the place he most wanted to be. But he is still with us. Now his world has become very small. He stays near his empty box by the heater in the kitchen. But on warmer days, he goes out and sits on the top step, turning his head this way and that, listening to small sounds like the flight of a bird.

As he sits there calmly waiting for the end, I do not give him pity. He would hate that as much as being carried across the brook. Instead I am grateful to him. Marco has shown me how to face trouble and how to best it with courage.

WHAT HAPPENED?   *summary*

Which three sentences help you remember
the main happenings in the story? Underline
each.

1. We called him Marco for short.
2. I ran out and found him lying in a
   ditch, his head thrown back, eyes
   open, unseeing.
3. Then I heard a soft moan.
4. The doctor said it was a stroke, but
   Marco wasn't about to give up.
5. I tried carrying him, but he wanted to
   be independent.

☞77 • *Each correct answer 10 points • My Score* _____

SEE THE CAT   *author's purpose*

To send you a good word picture of the cat,
which five of the following sentences did the
author use? Check ✔ each.

_____ 1. As a kitten, he loved to explore the
   house and go outside.
_____ 2. I heard a screech of car brakes.
_____ 3. One afternoon when we were both
   outside together, I noticed his strange
   walk—a stiff, careful trot.
_____ 4. I knew cats had a keen sense of smell,
   but when given food, Marco didn't
   know about it until he walked into it.
_____ 5. Marco raised each paw high, then put
   it forward slowly.

_____ 6. In his 15th year, he changed.

_____ 7. Or he'd chase windblown leaves in jerky gallops that made me laugh and almost cry.

⟜171 • Each correct answer 10 points • My Score _____

FEEL IT OUT   *inferences*

The author wrote the following words. What do they show about how he felt about Marco? Circle a, b or c.

1. How long had he been using his paw the way a blind person uses a cane?

  a. sympathetic b. angry c. tired

2. I'd watch with wonder as he made his way through the trees without ever bumping into anything.

  a. nosy b. timid c. admiring

⟜9 • Each correct answer 10 points • My Score _____
Perfect Total Score 100 • My Total Score _____

YOU TRY   *points of view*

Do you think "The Cat That Could" is a good title? Why or why not? What did the author learn from his pet? Give reasons for your answers.

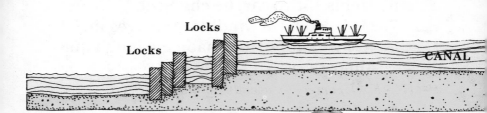

The Impossible Canal

by Thomas Fleming

Theodore Roosevelt, President of the United States, was angry. It was the night of February 12, 1907. On his desk was a letter from the chief engineer of the Panama Canal. John F. Stevens was quitting without warning, as had the engineer before him.

The dream of building a canal across the Isthmus of Panama was almost 400 years old. But the job had defeated all who tried it. France's Ferdinand de Lesseps had built the Suez Canal. Even he had been stopped by Panama's swamps, malarial jungle and 250

WATER LEVEL

Locks

Locks

Panama
Canal

83

days of rain each year. Now two of America's best engineers had also given up.

Some days later Roosevelt called in the Secretary of War, William Howard Taft. Roosevelt said, "I am going to put the canal in the charge of people who will stay on the job until I get tired of having them there. I shall turn it over to the army." That same evening, 49-year-old Major George Goethals (GO-thals) of the Army Engineers was called to the White House. By midnight he had accepted responsibility for one of the greatest building jobs ever attempted.

Arriving in the Canal Zone, Goethals told workers they were the army of Panama. He said, "The enemy we will fight is the Culebra (koo-LEE-bra) Cut. Let's get to work!"

There was an iron will in Goethals' voice. The workers soon learned that he acted with the same strong drive. One night a train engineer ignored warning lights that should have stopped his train. It crashed into the rear of a freight train and killed one of its crew. A Canal Zone court sentenced the engineer to one year in jail. His fellow engineers demanded that Goethals set the man free. If he

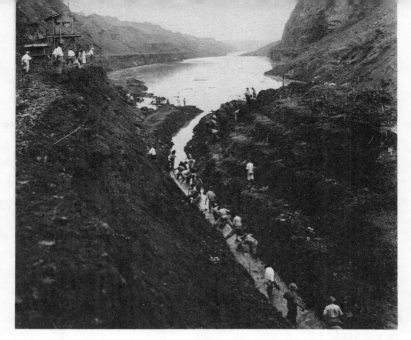

Workers digging on Culebra Cut

didn't do so in 24 hours, they would all stop working.

Not a word came back. Finally someone phoned Goethals for his answer. Goethals said, "The man is still in jail. Every person who fails to report for work tomorrow will be out of a job." At seven the next morning, every train was fully staffed.

Goethals would appear without warning to sit down with grimy workers and ask how they thought the work was going. Health officers were in charge of keeping yellow fever,

George Goethals at canal construction

malaria and other sicknesses under control. The officers often found him sitting at their desks, wanting to know why they were late for work.

Day after day, Goethals checked the 47-mile (75.64-kilometers) stretch of the Panama Railroad. Then he returned to his office. He would plan how to supply and direct his army, which soon numbered 40,000. Goethals dared them to blast, dig out and haul away more dirt and rock than they had ever dreamed possible. And they did.

Each of the Canal's 12 locks holds enough concrete to build Egypt's huge Pyramid of Cheops (KEE-ops). The Culebra Cut was a 300-foot-wide (91.44-meter), 120-foot-deep (36.58-meter) canyon blasted through bedrock. It kept 60 locomotives, each pulling 20 to 30 rock-filled cars, roaring in and out of the Cut all day.

Again and again, the rock walls of the Cut would break at the bottom. Thousands of tons of dirt and clay would come sliding down. Goethals would stare for some time and say, "Dig it out again!"

At 9:15 a.m., on August 15, 1914, a Panama Railroad ship cleared the Gatun (geh-TOON) Locks at the Atlantic end of the Canal. It moved smoothly across Gatun Lake to Culebra Cut. On it were officers of Panama and the U. S. and other important guests. But not George Goethals. He chose to ride along the shore in his yellow car, checking the teams of people he had trained to run the locks.

Visitors cheered as the ship churned past them. The 400-year-old dream of bridging the Isthmus of Panama had come true, thanks to George Goethals.

The opening of the Panama Canal

WHAT'S THE SCORE? *skimming*

Skim the story. Then underline the fact that will help you recall the story.

1. The dream of building a canal across the Isthmus of Panama was almost (a. 100, b. 200, c. 400) years old.

2. Goethals was asked to build the Panama Canal by (a. President Theodore Roosevelt, b. Secretary of War William Howard Taft, c. France's Ferdinand de Lesseps).

3. Day after day, Goethals checked the (a. 10-, b. 23-, c. 47-) mile stretch of the Panama railroad.

4. The Panama Canal has (a. 4, b. 8, c. 12) locks.

5. The Panama Canal was finished in (a. 1914, b. 1920, c. 1936).

☞*135 • Each correct answer 10 points • My Score* _____

DIG OUT THE ANSWER *supporting details*

Three of the statements below about Goethals are true. Check ✔ each.

_____ 1. He was a major in the Army Engineers.

_____ 2. He was the first engineer for the Panama Canal.

_____ 3. He was always late for work.

_____ 4. He dared the workers to work harder than they had ever dreamed possible.

_____ 5. When the Canal was finished, he personally checked up on the workers he had trained to run the locks.

☞ 76 • *Each correct answer 10 points* • *My Score* _____

YOU TALKING TO ME? *characterization*

Match each statement below with the person who said it. Put each letter in the space provided.

a. Theodore Roosevelt   b. George Goethals

_____ "Every person who fails to report for work tomorrow will be out of a job."
_____ "I shall turn it over to the Army."

☞ 3 • *Each correct answer 10 points* • *My Score* _____
Perfect Total Score 100 • *My Total Score* _____

YOUR TURN *paragraph meaning*

Which paragraph in the story best shows that George Goethals was a strong leader? Explain.

Glenda's Long Lonely Swim

by Frank Sargeant

In the storm-racked blackness of the Gulf of Mexico, the slim 23-year-old woman swam alone. The wind-whipped waves pounded her. Land was more than ten miles (16 kilometers) off. Fourteen hours in the water had tired her out. She began to fear that she could not last out the night.

There had been no hint of danger that sunny August afternoon when Glenda Lennon slipped into the calm, beautiful water to look at fish. Her husband, Robert, kept watch from their small boat. It was anchored in the channel five miles (8 kilometers) off Homosassa, Florida. When the tide runs out in that spot, the water runs fast along the channel. About 15 minutes after Glenda entered the water, she felt the current sweeping her away.

Robert dived off the boat to help her. A few swift strokes brought them together. But as Robert later remembered, "I could not pull Glenda against the current. With her diving mask, snorkel and swim fins, she was safe for a while. I decided to try for the boat alone."

For more than an hour, Robert fought against the outgoing tide. Finally he climbed on board the boat. He raced the boat to the west toward where he had left Glenda. The shrimp boats from Homosassa heard his radio calls for help and joined the search.

In a few hours, the area was alive with searchlights from fishing and pleasure boats. But Glenda was nowhere to be found.

Glenda fully believed Robert would soon return in their boat. But hours passed, and she became more and more frightened.

As the sun went down, she remembered stories of shark attacks in the outer Gulf. "I became thirsty, but I knew I could not drink the seawater. The storm that had been building up broke with a roar. Icy rain came down in sheets. I was cold and sleepy."

When the storm ended, Glenda just couldn't stay awake any longer. She cradled her face on the sea and fell asleep. Her snorkel remained above water, giving her air as she dozed. When she woke up, the sky had cleared.

Twenty miles (32 kilometers) to the east, the searching party gathered at Homosassa. The group felt there was little hope left.

But one man among them believed that he still might be able to find Glenda. Duncan MacRae, a silent man who ran a boat yard in Homosassa, had spent many years studying the Gulf. He knew these waters perhaps better than any person along the coast.

In the morning's first light, Duncan put out in a small, fast boat with two other men.

He headed out to where Robert's boat had been anchored. Afterwards he explained, "I let my boat drift as I studied the waves. By my figuring, most of the search had taken place too far inshore. After a brief calculation, I raced my boat west-north-west."

Within the next half hour, Duncan repeatedly rushed down on shining objects, only to find cans, bottles, crab-trap floats. Duncan began to believe they might have by-passed Glenda in the choppy sea. A

moment later, a thin, pale arm rose above a wave. "I can't believe it—she's alive," one of the men murmured.

When the boat neared Glenda, Duncan stopped the motor. As the boat slid by, Duncan caught one of Glenda's wrists in his powerful right hand. He pulled her over the side of the boat. Glenda Lennon's long swim was ended.

Too weak to move, she began to cry, and there were tears on the faces of all three men. They wrapped her in blankets, and at top speed, the boat headed east. The first boat they sighted at the shore was the Lennons', with Robert at the wheel. As Duncan pulled beside it, Robert leaped from his boat and landed beside Glenda. She had been swimming more than 20 hours and had lost 20 pounds (9 kilograms). Glenda had struggled against the sea and had won.

RESCUE THE ORDER   *sequence*

In what order do these sentences belong? Put 1 before the sentence that should be first, 2 before the sentence that should be next, and so on.

_____ But one man among them believed that he still might be able to save her.

_____ Within a few hours, the area was alive with searchlights from boats.

_____ There was no hint of danger when Glenda slipped into the water that day.

_____ After Glenda entered the water, she felt the current sweeping her away.

_____ A thin, pale arm rose above a wave.

167 · Each correct answer 5 points · My Score _____

SEA TALK   *cause/effect*

Read each pair of sentences below. Underline the sentence that gives the reason for what the other sentence says.

1. a. She began to fear that she could not last out the night.
   b. Hours in the water had tired her.
2. a. With her diving equipment on, she was safe for a while.
   b. Robert decided to try for the boat.
3. a. She cradled her face on the sea.
   b. Glenda could stay awake no longer.

4. a. Duncan MacRae had studied the Gulf.
   b. He knew more about these waters than almost anyone.

5. a. She had been swimming for 20 hours.
   b. Glenda had struggled against the sea and won.

☞130 • Each correct answer 10 points • My Score _____

SEARCH FOR THE ANSWER *fact/opinion*

Write A before each sentence that tells a fact,
B before each sentence that shows a feeling.

_____ And now she was beginning to fear that she could not last the night.

_____ The Lennons' boat was anchored in the channel five miles off Homosassa.

_____ The shrimp boats from Homosassa heard Robert's radio calls for help.

_____ Glenda fully believed Robert would soon return in their boat.

_____ The group felt there was little hope.

☞129 • Each correct answer 5 points • My Score _____
Perfect Total Score 100 • My Total Score _____

OUT TO SEA *points of view*

If you were Glenda, how might you have prevented the frightening experience?